FOR A FLY FISHERMAN WHO HAS EVERYTHING

A Funny Fly-Fishing Book

Team Golfwell and Bruce Miller

This is the tenth book in the series, *For People Who Have Everything.*

Cover by Queen Graphics. All images are from Creative Commons or Shutterstock

ISBN 9798840359839 (Amazon hardcover)

ISBN 9798840359952 (Amazon paperback)

ISBN 9781991048080 (Ingram EPUB)

ISBN 9781991048097 (Ingram Spark hardback)

ISBN 9781991048103 (Ingram Spark paperback)

Outwit. "There he stands, draped in more equipment than a telephone lineman, trying to outwit an organism with a brain no bigger than a breadcrumb, and getting licked in the process."

    -- Paul O'Neil

I like to catch fish. "Our tradition of the sport of fly fishing began when there was that first man who sneaked away to the creek when the tribe did not really need fish."

    -- Roderick Haig-Brown, about modern fishing, *"A River Never Sleeps"* 1946

How long have people been fly fishing? "When man first began to fish, he used a Gorge rather than a hook (hooks came later). A Gorge consisted of a piece of wood, bone, or stone that had been sharpened at both ends. The earliest hooks were made from bone about 3000 years ago in the south of Europe. They were of a simple design, but like modern-day hooks. Early references to fishing with rod and line can be found on the ancient Egyptian tomb paintings." [1]

Other than a few fragmented references little was written on fly fishing until The Treatyse on Fysshynge with an Angle was published (1496) within The Boke of Saint Albans attributed to Dame Juliana Berners. The book contains instructions on rod, line, hook making, and dressings for different flies to use at different times of the year. By the 15th century, rods of approximately fourteen feet in length with a twisted line attached at their tips were probably used in England. [2]

However, "It was not until the end of the 15th century that fly fishing was practiced as a sport by the upper classes of England. An exact date when fishing and fly fishing were first practiced for sport is difficult to establish. However, an article entitled "The Treatyse of Fysshynge with an Angle" which by tradition was penned by the known Dame Juliana Berner, prioress of a nunnery near London, and published in the Book of St Albans in 1496 is often used to date the birth of sport-fishing." [3]

Fast-growing. "Nothing grows faster than a fish from when it bites until it gets away."

-- Anon.

Don't need to catch fish. "If catching fish is your only objective, you are either new to the game or too narrowly focused on measurable results."

— David Stuver, "Familiar Waters: A lifetime of fly-fishing Montana"

What's important. "If people concentrated on the really important things of life, there'd be a shortage of fly-fishing poles."

-- Doug Larson

Alien abduction. A man wades into a river and stands near another man fly fishing who has a large trout on his line reeling it in. He lifts a massive trout, then immediately releases it.

"That was a nice one. Don't you want to keep it?"

The man reflected and said, "I don't keep what I catch. I just stick a barbed hook in its face and yank it and lift it out of the water gasping and wriggling. Then I rip the hook out and throw it back in, leaving it to wonder if that was an alien abduction or what kind of God would allow such a thing."

Horsehair? Originally fly-fishing lines were commonly made of braided horsehair. [4]

Fish and chips. One day while driving home from his fishing trip in the pouring rain, a man got a flat tire outside of a monastery. A monk came out and invited the man inside to have dinner and to spend the night. The stranded motorist gladly accepted the monk's offer.

That evening the man had a wonderful dinner of fish and chips. He decided to compliment the chef.

Entering the kitchen, the man asked the cook, "Are you the fish friar?"

"No," the chef replied, "I'm the chip monk."

Golden rule. The fisherman's golden rule: the one that got away is always bigger than the one you gotta weigh.

-- Anon.

Not easy. "To him, all good things - trout as well as eternal salvation- come by grace, and grace comes by art, and art does not come easy."

-- Norman Maclean from the book "A River Runs Through It"

Sloppy. Q. What do you call a crayfish with a sloppy hiding place.

A. Slobster.

Religion. "If fishing is like religion, then fly-fishing is high church."

-- Tom Brokaw

Not really casting. "…with a fly rod, anglers are not casting to a fish; rather to a circle of dreams: ripples that spread into every aspect of their lives."

— Fennel Hudson

Commitment. "Committing to being a fly-only angler, makes me feel like I'm washing away the grime from my fishing tackle to reveal the beauty of what lies beneath."

— Fennel Hudson

American Fly Fishing. In the late 19th century, American anglers, such as Theodore Gordon in the Catskill Mountains of New York, began using fly tackle to fish the region's brook trout-rich streams such as the Beaverkill and Willowick Creek. Many of these early American fly anglers also developed new fly patterns and wrote extensively about their sport, increasing the popularity of fly fishing in the region and in the United States as a whole. [5]

Charles F. Orvis opened a tackle shop in Manchester, Vermont, in 1856. His 1874 fly reel was described by reel historian Jim

Brown as the "benchmark of American reel design," the first fully modern fly reel. [6]

Mary Orvis Marbury

In 1892 Mary Orvis Marbury created the first book of fly patterns. The legacy of Mary Marbury, through her book and her leadership in Orvis's commercial fly-tying operation, is the standardization of American fly patterns. Her book, "Favorite Flies and Their Histories" remains one of the most significant landmarks in American fly-tying literature. It's considered by most fly fishers as the standard reference on flies in its era. [7]

Learning. "Many go fishing all their lives without knowing that it is not fish they are after."

    -- Henry David Thoreau

Imaginative excuses. A man came home late, and his wife was a little peeved and asked him to explain.

He said, "Well you see Honey I went fishing and thought I would just do a little bank fishing, got my gear out of the car and walked aways to the water. I threw my line in and oh boy I pulled in a big catfish. I then found out I forgot to bring my fish basket. So, I just threw the catfish behind me under a tree. I baited up again and in a little while I caught one of those ole dogfishes. I didn't want to put it back in the water, so I threw it under the tree too. I baited up again and sat there waiting for my next catch." His wife was still listening

"Suddenly, I heard such a noise and when I looked that dogfish and that catfish were in a fight and that dogfish chased the catfish up that tree and I had to sit there all day before I caught a sawfish to saw that tree down to get my catfish."

Fills your senses and hooks your soul. "Granddad always said the best things about fishing were beyond the senses. He said the mountains, rivers and fish were the center of why you were there, but not the heart, that the heart was in those pure moments in and around the fishing, or rather what was on the other side of those moments that can only be felt, not told because words were not up to the job. That's what hooked your soul."

— J.C. Bonnell, Burnt Tree Fork

The World Fly Fishing Tournament. The International Fly-Fishing Federation or "Fédération

Internationale de Peche Sportive Mouche" is the fly-fishing arm of CIPS (Confédération Internationale de la Pêche Sportive), founded in Rome in 1952, is behind the World Fly Fishing Tournament with six rounds -- three hours of fly fishing held at five different geographical locations mixture of lakes and rivers to test all skills. [8]

All fish caught are measured for length, rather than weight and are returned to the water alive. Points are awarded to the most successful anglers and section points per round according to placing, with the winner receiving one point, and the lowest overall score wins. [9] Finland is the current championship team.

World fly fishing championships were inaugurated by the CIPS in 1981. The most team titles are five by Italy, 1982–4, 1986, 1992. [10]

Enjoying the environment. "…the things we desire, or need may kill us. This can be another reason to take a fly rod in hand and enjoy the environment in and around a stream, and for brief periods of time leave behind all the things you cannot change."

— David Stuver, Familiar Waters: A lifetime of fly-fishing Montana

Talking to God. "Some go to church and think about fishing, others go fishing and think about God."

--Tony Blake

Leaving the tensions of life. "Eli returned to the river and paused for a moment midstream. His feet were balanced upon uneven stones. The current tumbled around him. The canyon walls were steep and jagged and solid. The colors beneath the surface stirred and glittered.

He wanted to hold his face under water and breathe in their beauty. He dipped his fingers into the snow-cold transient texture and felt a tingle. He closed his eyes to see this sensation clearly. He breathed.

He put his hand up to his face and felt the freshness enter his soul. Water droplets dripped from his skin and returned to the river. He opened his eyes as if they were separate from his body, separate from the tension of life, distant from any distraction. He breathed."

— Daniel J. Rice, "This Side of a Wilderness"

Bad day. A wife was talking to her neighbor after returning from a fishing trip with her husband. "I did everything all wrong again today.

"What did you do?" the neighbor asks,

- I forgot his lucky fishing lure at home.

- I talked too much and too loudly.

- I used the wrong bait.

- I reeled in too soon and WORST of all I caught more fish than he did.

Nature of life. "Fly fishing is a contemplative experience that embodies the truth of nature and the nature of life"

— Michael Vincent Stagnitta

Feature film. Q. Why was the movie about fly fishing a box office flop?

A. Bad casting.

A toast before fishing.

Here's to the fish that we may catch,

So large that any of us,

When talking of it afterward,

Will never need to lie.

Trout pun. Ever seen a fish astronaut?

It went to trouter space.

A few fish facts.

- A biologist who studies fish is called an ichthyologist.

- The most poisonous fish in the world is the Stonefish.

- The more sardines that are placed in a can, the greater the profit as sardine oil costs more than sardines.

- Minnows have teeth in their stomach; the better to digest their food.

- The sturgeon is considered the largest of all freshwater fish and have weighed in at 2,250 pounds.

- All the sturgeon (the fish from which we get caviar) caught in British waters are property of Elizabeth II, Queen of England.

- Atlantic salmon can leap as high as 15 feet.

- The largest known fish in the sea is the whale shark. It weighs up to 20 tons and can grow to a length of 40 feet.

- Fish can get seasick when kept aboard a rolling ship just as much as people.

- The red fire-fish can fly and emits sounds like a crow.

Answering machine. A reporter goes to see an inventor who claims to have invented a machine that can answer any question. The reporter is asked to speak his question into the microphone and the machine will answer it with 100% accuracy.

Skeptical but curious the reporter starts easy, "Where is my mother?"

The machine bleeps and buzzes and then announces, "Your mother is at her book club, they have just reviewed To Kill a Mockingbird and are now having sandwiches."

Amazed the reporter calls his mother and confirms she is indeed enjoying a sandwich at her book club having just reviewed To Kill a Mockingbird.

Now he really wants to test the machine, he asks "Where is my father?"

The machine bleeps and buzzes and then announces, "Your father is fishing in Scotland."

"Ha! Gotcha! Says the reporter to the inventor. My father has been dead for fifteen years."

Confused, the inventor suggests that the reporter asks the question differently.

Alright then, the reporter says, "Where is my mother's husband?"

The machine bleeps and buzzes and then announces, "Your mother's husband has been dead for fifteen years. Your father just caught an eight-pound trout."

Many reasons for fishing. If I fished only to capture fish, my fishing trips would have ended long ago.

-- Zane Grey

Offer. Someone offered to take me fly fishing, but I turned them down.

I like to keep it reel.

No more troubles. "Finally, Gunner spoke, his voice so fluid and moving, it could have come from the river itself. 'I once heard a poem about angling. It says when you send out your line, it is like you cast out your troubles to let the current carry them away. I keep casting.'"

— Clare Vanderpool, "Navigating Early"

Questions. A father and son went fishing one summer day. While they were out in their boat, the boy suddenly became curious about the world around him. He asked his father, "Dad, how does this boat float?"

The father replied, "Don't rightly know son."

A little later, the boy looked at his father and asked, "Dad, how do fish breath underwater?"

Once again the father replied, "Don't rightly know son."

A little later the boy asked his father, "Dad, why is the sky blue?"

Again, the father replied, "Don't rightly know son."

Finally, the boy asked his father, "Dad, do you mind my asking you all of these questions?"

The father replied, "Of course not, son. If you don't ask questions, you never learn nothin'."

Consider this. "Give a man a fish and he'll have food for a day. Teach a man to fish and... he must buy bamboo rods, graphite reels, monofilament lines, neoprene waders, creels, tackleboxes, lures, flies, spinners, worm rigs, slip sinkers, offset hooks, Gore-Tex hats, 20 pocket vests, fish finders, depth sounders, radar, boats, trailers, global positioning systems, coolers, and six-packs. And this, my friends, is how love f*cks up your life."

— Beck Anderson, "Use Somebody"

Crime. "Lots of people committed crimes during the year who would not have done so if they had been fishing. The increase of crime is among those deprived of the regenerations that impregnate the mind and character of the fisherman."

-- Herbert Hoover

Fish story. "Don't tell fish stories where the people know you; but particularly, don't tell them where they know the fish."

-- Mark Twain

Haunted. "Eventually, all things merge into one, and a river runs through it. The river was cut by the world's great flood and runs over rocks from the basement of time. On some of the rocks are timeless raindrops. Under the rocks are the words, and some of the words are theirs. I am haunted by waters."

-- Norman Maclean

Privacy respected. "There are only two occasions when Americans respect privacy, especially in Presidents. Those are prayer and fishing."

-- Herbert Hoover

Born fishermen. "All Americans believe that they are born fishermen. For a man to admit a distaste for fishing would be like denouncing motherlove or hating moonlight."

-- John Steinbeck

Montana. "My soul lives in Montana. It's where I fly-fish for trout."

-- Henry Winkler

Talking trout. "There's no taking trout with dry breeches."

-- Miguel de Cervantes

Sometimes you need to work. "Sure, I could retire anytime. I don't need to work for money. But retire to what? Sitting around the pool reading? Or even trout fishing. I love trout fishing, and I go every time I get a chance. But a man with pride in his profession need to work."

-- Van Heflin, Actor

Pristine. "The traveler fancies he has seen the country. So, he has, the outside of it at least; but the angler only sees the inside. The angler only is brought close, face to face with the flower and bird and insect life of the rich riverbanks, the only part of the landscape where the hand of man has never interfered."

    -- Charles Kingsley

Addicted. "I grew up in Florida, started fishing with my dad going down to the Everglades and around the state, plus some offshore stuff for sails and wahoo - but I never really got the bug until my husband, and I went float fishing on the Snake River at Jackson Hole for trout - I've been pretty much addicted ever since."

-- Shannon Bream, American Journalist

Wife doesn't want husband to fish. A man loved to fish and enjoyed his occasional fishing trips. His jealous wife nagged and complained he loved fishing more than her. She made his life miserable every chance she got she found things to annoy him by hiding his fishing gear, turning his truck headlights on and leaving them on overnight leaving a dead battery and delaying him in the morning to go fishing.

She kept hounding him and finally put her foot down and told him he couldn't fish anymore. He told her he was still going to go fishing now and then.

She got mad and packed his bags and told him to get out!

As he walked to the door she yelled, "I hope you die a long, slow, painful death."

He turned around and said, "So, you want me to stay?"

Fly fisherman needs help. A widower sits quietly in a darkened room having a séance with a psychic medium.

The medium says, "We have reached your wife."

The man opens his eyes wide and says, "Ask her where she put my fly rod. I've searched everywhere."

Stress. "Stress is caused by not fishing enough."

> -- Anon.

My fish was soooh big!

How big was it?

- That fish was so freeking huge, that when I took a picture of it, my camera started smoking due to an overloaded memory card.

- You guys should have seen it! The smallest spots on this brown trout were so huge, I thought one of them might open up and envelop the earth like a black hole on Star Trek.

- On my way back to the boat launch, I had to store my boat IN the fish to get back.

- As I was floating down the river yesterday, I thought my boat got stuck on the bottom of the river, turns out it was a fish pushing the boat out of its way so it could eat my fly.

- I hooked a trout the other day that was such a blatant river pig, that its shadow weighed close to ten pounds!

- On my way back from the trout stream yesterday a group of anti-whaling protesters had gathered on my front lawn. They assumed the brown I caught was some type of porpoise.

- Speaking of porpoises. I drove by a daycare on my way back from the river. All the kids hit the ground in tears. They thought it was "Shamu the great white whale" hanging out of my boat.

- After Wall Street heard about that trout I hooked yesterday, the commodity price of fish tanked to an all-time low. Turns out I crashed the market due to a surplus of fish meat.

- I caught a trout so big, the picture of it was three pounds. The negative was a pound. We went into the lake to eat it rather than bring it home.

- I knew that fish I pulled in looked familiar, I had seen him last year on the hit show "the biggest loser" -- he got kicked off because he was beyond the help of the personal trainers.

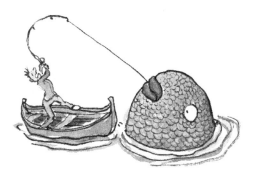

Fish Riddles.

Q. Why are fish so gullible?

A. They fall for things, hook, line, and sinker.

Q. What kind of music should you listen to while fishing?

A. Something catchy!

Q. Why did Batman and Robin quit going fishing together?

A. Because Robin ate all the worms!

Q. What do you call a fish that practices medicine?

A. Sturgeon.

Q. Why are fish so lucky?

A. They seize every oper- tuna – ty

Q. What is a fish's least favorite day of the week?

A. Fryday.

Q. Where do fish keep their money?

A. In the Riverbank.

Q. What did the trout say to the bass?

A. "You're my bass friend. No trout about it!"

(If you can think of a better fish pun, let minnow.)

Worm. "Fly-fishing may be a very pleasant amusement; but angling or float fishing I can only compare to a stick and a string, with a worm at one end and a fool at the other."

-- Samuel Johnson

Costs of fishing. Two fishermen travel 100 miles to try out a new fishing spot. They buy a variety of bait and lures and rent a boat.

After a long day of fishing, the two fishermen return to the dock. The first fisherman pulls their only catch from the live well, a scrawny bass just legal size. He says, "Boy! This fish cost us about $75."

The second fisherman says, "Well it's a good thing we didn't catch any more."

Some reasons why fly fishing doesn't get old.

- Fly fishing never gets old because it is a challenge that anglers set for themselves.

- Because, at worst, fishing can be great fun it induces relaxation, calm and peace.

- At best, it's a combination of fishing and catching, which adds an element of the rush of fighting, landing, and eating fish, if you're not doing "catch & release."

- Fishing is also an agreement. Each angler has a set of goals and rules for attaining those goals. Perhaps it's partly tied to personal image - the angler is assuming a role, which will be played out according to personal rules.

- Fishing success is never guaranteed - anglers have to think, plan and work to be successful.

- There is much more to fishing than "just going fishing." The time spent "on the water" is never wasted -- it's therapeutic and brings the angler in touch with deep human historical roots that reach back several hundred thousand years (or more!) and perhaps during 99.6% of human evolution.

- Finally, it never gets old because fishing helped humanity survive over the ages to the present day.

Real meaning. "In the lexicon of the fly-fishermen, the words rise and hooked connote the successful and desirable climax; landing a fish is purely anticlimax."

-- Vincent C. Marinaro, 1950

Lots of bites. "I went fishing with my new flyrod and got plenty of bites."

"Trout?"

"No, mosquitoes."

Flopping. "When I look at my daily schedule, I feel like a trout flopping about on a dock, drowning in the air. Some people are ruthless with their schedules. Not me. I wing it."

-- Douglas Coupland, *Canadian novelist*

A true fly-fishing story and how it began. "In November 2020 I was invited last minute to fly to New Orleans to fish with a guy from high school that became a fishing guide. I've been freshwater fishing since I was young and have always lived in the Midwest, but never picked up a fly rod.

"We were hammering giant bull reds one after another with swimbaits on gear, and my friend suggested I try the fly. I went from full confidence to clueless. I think I was using a really fast 10wt at first, then switched to an 8wt H3 with a fairly heavy shrimp fly, and there was some decent wind.

"I eventually managed to make a decent cast and caught a nice black drum, my first fish on a fly. From that point, I was determined to become as fluent with the fly as I am with the gear.

"A year and a few months later I now own 4 fly rods, have fished the Florida Keys for tarpon, Belize and Bahamas for bonefish, and a 5-day Alaska rafting trip for kings, grayling, and trout.

"Bonefish, and fishing the flats in general, is what really got me. Just feels like the peak of what fishing is all about for me. Hoping to plan some more fun trips soon, with permit and bonefish being at the top of my list."

-- Anon.

Bonefish

Four things about fly-fishing.

1. It takes a lot of thought. You must consider, the river, current, eddies, trout feeding patterns, where to place the fly so it can drift naturally, and more.

2. It's a workout. Walking through waist-deep water, against strong currents, over the slippery, rocky riverbed is about one of the best workouts you can get. Plus, swinging that rod back and forth really works that casting arm.

3. The views. You see parts of the wild that only the river can take you to and that you might not be able to access if it weren't for walking through the water. You get a whole new magical view of nature from a perspective that you wouldn't get otherwise.

4. All in all, it's exciting, frustrating, immensely satisfying, and enormously rewarding. It tends to not get old and once you try it, you'll be hooked!

Thugs. "A street thug and a paid killer are professionals -- beasts of prey, if you will, who have dissociated themselves from the rest of humanity and can now see human beings in the same way that trout fishermen see trout."

-- Willard Gaylin, *Clinical Professor of Psychiatry Emeritus at Columbia College of Physicians and Surgeons and co-founder, of The Hastings Center, an independent research institute focused on bioethics.*

Fly Fishing spots.

"I don't always tell people where I fly fish, but when I do it's a lie."

Here is a list of what most consider the best fly-fishing spots in the world for trout, bonefish, permit, salmon and other fish.

- The Bahamas has some of the best fly fishing in the world for bonefish. Close to the US, you can take a short flight to Bimini for excellent bonefishing, especially during July. The nearby Bahamian Island, Andros Island, is excellent as well.

- Beginning in December in the Southern hemisphere, the Tongariro National Park (a World Heritage site) in New Zealand is the best time of year for people to get into their waders in the crystal-clear waters where it is easy to spot trout swimming near you or even more so from most bridges over these pristine waters. For those who enjoy hiking, the Tongariro Alpine Crossing in Tongariro National Park is considered one of the best one-day hikes in the world and considered by some as like walking on the moon with its remarkable volcanic landscape.

- At the northern end of the Bahamas, the Abacos has large and productive bonefish flats on the western side of Great Abaco.

- Looking for adventure? Alphonse Island in the Seychelles is an uninhabited Indian Ocean atoll known for bonefish, permit and a host of exotic game fish such as milkfish and giant trevally.

- Mexico's Ascension Bay (about one hundred miles south of Cancun) offers anglers flats loaded with bones and permit, and mangrove estuaries laden with snook and tarpon.

- Exmouth, Western Australia with its large flats, including Ningaloo Lagoon, is known as one of the best spots for fly fishers. Pacific permit, bonefish, trevallies, queenfish, milkfish, giant parrotfish, and more inshore fish.

- The lower 100 miles of the Deschutes River in north-central Oregon, is known throughout the world for redside rainbow trout and summer steelhead trout. The best sections on the lower Deschutes River are known to be upstream from the milky White River located just below Maupin upriver to the Pelton Dam near Warm Springs.

- Ixtapa, Guatemala is one of the best fly-fishing spots in the world for offshore anglers looking for sailfish. In fact, some say it is the only place where a fly fisherman can hook sailfish.

- You should bring all your tackle if you ever visit Jupiter Inlet, Florida which has a variety of game fish for fly fishers along Atlantic beaches just off this southeast Florida inlet. It's a spot for fly fishermen to land spinner sharks, jumbo jack crevalle, cobia, and more. In the summer, tarpon and snook are also known to be available.

- Montauk, New York for some of the best fly-rod action. On Long Island, this area is active from the middle of spring through the middle of summer, in clear shallow flats around Gardiner's Island and in Peconic Bay for stripers and bluefish.

- Turneffe, Belize for bonefish, permit and tarpon and other game fish. There are shallow reefs around expansive flats and it's year-round for wade fishing and tarpon in the summer.

- Try the Beaverhead River to wading the Spring Creeks in Paradise Valley in Montana for trout.

- Canada has world-class trout fishing across the entire country on the Albany River, Elk River, Old Man River, Wigwam River, Tree River, Bow River, and many more. The trout in Canada usually run above average in size and are good for steady dry fly fishing, good hatches, and healthy trout.

- Not very populated, Andros Island in the Bahamas is known for some of the best bonefishing in the world. Also, the Barrier Reef and Tongue of the Sea is the third largest barrier reef in the world measuring more than 140 miles long and lies just off the shores of Andros Island. The reef has almost every variety of barrier fish species.

- New Zealand is one of the world's great fly-fishing countries where trout are plentiful throughout the North and South Island. Lakes, rivers, backcountry streams and spring creeks all have opportunities to fish for brown and rainbow trout. In the South Island, you can also fish for salmon in many places.

- For peace and purity, Alaska has amazing spots on rivers originating in Bristol Bay – from Katmai National Park, Lake Iliamna, and Wood Tikchik State Park. Nature hasn't changed these spots in centuries. The spots in Bristol Bay are accessible by plane.

- The Patagonia region in Argentina features fly-fishing in areas such as San Martin, Rio Pico, Junin, Esquel, and the southernmost tip, Tierra Del Fuego. The rivers Rio Traful, Rio Malleo, the Limay, Rio Grande, Rio Pico, and Chimehuin River produce abundant hatches and food sources for trout and are also highly pristine and known for trout.

- Of course, there is England for one of the chalk streams where the sport began for brown trout and best to go when the mayfly hatches, usually toward the end of May. Mayflies are large, green insects. There are wild streams in Dorset, the special chalk streams of Yorkshire and the limestone rivers of the Derbyshire National Park.

There are so many magical places!

Quality excuses. "The difference between fly fishers and worm dunkers is the quality of their excuses."

-- Anon.

Memories. "Whether I caught fish or not, just the thrill of rolling out that line and watching my fly turn over has been good enough for me. That and the hundreds of treasured memories I have of this wonderful sport."

-- Curt Gowdy

Meant to be. "Three-fourths of the Earth's surface is water, and one-fourth is land. It is quite clear that the good Lord intended us to spend triple the amount of time fishing as taking care of the lawn."

--Chuck Clark

How I began to enjoy fly-fishing, a true story.
This is a story you may find interesting.

"I started 30 odd years ago around age 10 with the dream of matching the hatch on trout streams and wading the flats for bonefish. As it so happens I had neither where I lived. I practiced my art (fly tying included) on bluegill of the local ponds with an occasional trip to the mountains for trout.

"I've seen a lot of innovations and adopted many of them along the way, synthetic material for fly tying, bead heads, high stick nymphing, euro nymphing, mono rigs, foam, etc.

"A few years ago, I walked back to the parking area, alongside one of Pennsylvania's famous limestones, with a man who proclaimed, "Dry fly fishing is the only REAL fly fishing." At the time I thought he was crazy, I thought doesn't he like catching fish? You can just throw a bead head nymph on catch fish all day or lob a heavy streamer and catch a fish if a lifetime or simply swing a wet fly.

"Now some people talk about forgoing fly lines altogether and I tie flies with a ⅛ oz of weight on them and think to myself "Maybe that old crotchety fisherman was righter than I gave him credit for."

-- Anon.

Listening. "Listen to the sound of the river and you will get trout."

-- Irish proverb

What makes a good fly fisherman?

"A good fly fisherman knows that fishing is not the same as catching. It's a willingness to endure fishing in all conditions, times of days, days of the week and so on. It can be frustrating, but loved, nevertheless.

"It is your Zen. Your happy place. Very few things in life can make time stop like when I'm watching a well-cast fly dead drift over a riffle where I know a fish should be holding. That split second between bite, and hook set. The 10 seconds it takes to reel it in that feels like an hour.

"Loving all aspects of fishing, not just catching, will make anyone a better angler.

"A good fly fisherman knows where to fish and when the fish are feeding.

"There is a saying that is so true – 'Ninety of fish are caught by 10% of fishermen.' A good fisherman is one who takes in the tides, wind, moon phase, fishing spot, bait, lure, and has the right gear to the target species sought.

"It takes the right kind of fishing to achieve a good balance between rod reel and line along with the knowledge and ability to read and study the water tides, kinds of fish and baits. The best fishermen know the right rig set up and know at least 5 types of knots and have the knowledge to join braided to mono or vice versa. They also are passionate about fishing and realize that every cast is important. They have a positive mind, patience and a willingness to learn new tactics and skills from other anglers. They are willing to ask questions without feeling ashamed or shy to learn new ways of fishing and share opinions on everything about fishing. They understand and realize no one is perfect but enjoy the pursuit of perfection and that perfect catch."

-- Anon.

Fly fishing fan. "There is no greater fan of fly fishing than the worm."

> -- Patrick McManus

How to determine if someone has little fishing experience?

- Uses a plastic worm balled up on a hook with a bobber on the rig.

- Has a baitcasting reel on a spinning rod.

- Underhand casts with a spin casting outfit.

- Gets disinterested after 10 minutes and starts feeding ducks.

- Sprays himself with fish attractant spray.

- Thinks Jimmy Houston is from Texas.

- Has a 2-foot Disney-themed fishing rod and reel.

- Uses bread for bait.

- Asks if you have got any "nibbles."

- Marvels at your skills.

Bragging rights. "Bragging may not bring happiness, but no man having caught a large fish goes home through an alley."

> -- Anon.

A pastor's wife walks into a butcher shop.

She sees the most perfect-looking cut of fish in the display case and asks the butcher what kind of fish it is.

"That's Dam Fish," he replies.

"I beg your PARDON?!" the lady says, "I am a good Christian woman, and I would kindly ask you not to use that kind of language."

The butcher explains, "Oh no ma'am, I'm not using profanity. Dam Fish is what we call the especially delicious filets we get from the big trout caught down by the dam."

The woman apologizes for the misunderstanding, buys the filet, and goes home.

Later that evening, her husband comes home from work and asks, "What is that Heavenly smell?"

"That's Dam Fish," she replies.

"Honey! What would the congregation think if they knew their pastor's wife was speaking in such a way?"

"Oh no honey, I would never!" She responds, "They call it Dam Fish because it's a special filet from one of the big trout caught down by the dam."

She finishes dinner and they sit down at the table with their two beautiful children. They join hands and say grace. The husband carves the fish filets, takes some for himself, then passes the plate to his son.

After taking his first bite, the husband says, "Honey, you've really outdone yourself. This Dam Fish is delicious!"

"Right on, Dad!" The son says, "Now could you pass the f*#king potatoes?"

In business. Q. What did the trout and the carpenter ant name their online business?

A. Efishant.

Gift. "The finest gift you can give to any fisherman is to put a good fish back, and who knows if the fish that you caught isn't someone else's gift to you?"

> -- Lee Wulff

Fly box. "I investigate ... my fly box and think about all the elements I should consider in choosing the perfect fly: water temperature, what stage of development the bugs are in, what the fish are eating right now. Then I remember what a guide told me: 'Ninety percent of what a trout eats is brown and fuzzy and about five-eighths of an inch long.'"

> -- Allison Moir, *"Love the Man, Love the Fly Rod"*, in *A Different Angle: Fly Fishing Stories by Women*

Question. "Something is fishy about fly fishing. Do you really think fish are flying?"

-- Anon.

Irony. "I was dating a girl and her father hated me. I liked the girl but the only thing I had in common with her father was fishing but I was a bass fishing spin guy, and he was a fly only trout guy.

"He never took me fly fishing, but he did give me a tying lesson which got me interested. I went full in on everything fly fishing. I got so obsessed that his daughter broke up with me cause all I wanted to do was fly fish."

-- Anon.

Worth it. "Fishing is worth any amount of effort and any amount of expense to people who love it. And that's because in the end, you get such a large number of dreams per fish."

-- Ian Frazier, The Fish's Eye

Magic. "Fly-fishing is a magic way to recapture the rapture of solitude without the pangs of loneliness."

-- John D. Voelker

Solitary. "Fly-fishing is solitary, contemplative, misanthropic, scientific in some hands, poetic in others, and laced with conflicting aesthetic considerations. It's not even clear if catching fish is actually the point."

-- John Gierach

One that got away.

A fisherman, 'tween you and I

Will very seldom tell a lie---

Except when it is needed to

Describe the fish that left his view.

Lost phone and other strange tales

- A businessman who lost his mobile phone on a beach was amazed when it turned up - in the belly of a 25-pound cod.

- The blue-stoned class ring of Joe Richardson, engraved with his name, turned up inside an 8-pound bass 21 years after he lost it while fishing on Lake Sam Rayburn, USA. The finder has remained anonymous.

- A gold ring turned up inside the belly of a fish caught by an angler off Fort Victoria, near Yarmouth, Isle of Wight, UK.

- Biologists at the University of Manchester, England, want help in cracking their "miracle" discovery of three fish inside a sealed egg. The group found the duck egg in a small pond on a field trip to the French Alps and noticed something moving inside it. When they cracked open the shell, three live minnows were inside. They have enlisted the help of other experts, but despite their extensive combined knowledge, the biologists admit they are "baffled."

- The Dutchman Cor Stoop leaned over the side of his fishing boat, and his false teeth fell into the North Sea. He never thought that he'd see them again. Three months later another fisherman found the dentures inside the stomach of a cod.

I can't think like a fish so how do I improve my fishing? "You don't have to think like a fish, because they don't "think" as such -- they respond to stimuli. It's up to you to learn which of those stimuli you should learn how to read, and act on those. Such as locations in the river most likely to hold fish of the species you're after. The more you fish, the luckier you'll get. (Like the famous golfer said the more practice you do the luckier you'll get).

"You need to understand there's no quick way to learn, and experience will teach you.

"Reading about fishing rather than just the how-to will teach you gently rather than "How to Catch Fish Using These 5 Steps."

"Don't waste money on cheap tackle or new-fangled tackle. I mean fish have zero fashion sense. Advertising and marketing men stepped in years ago and suddenly people get persuaded to get special rods for this and that promising to work miracles. Talk to experienced fishermen on what they use and why they use them.

"You can't buy your way into being a better fisherman with a shinier rod, a zippier reel, a hyper-ultra-tapered fly line with the newest wonder coating... and so on.

"Buy a good pair of Polaroids. Not ones built especially for fishing, endorsed by some big fishing-name who got a fat cheque to say they're just the job. Get a good standard set, and not too dark either. Those will let you see through the surface reflection and should be always with you. If you wear glasses, consider getting a polarized pair.

"Understand that time beside the water isn't wasted and taking a camera along can be fun."

-- Anon.

Why I fish. "I fish not because I regard fishing as being terribly important, but because I suspect that so many of the other concerns of men are equally unimportant, and not nearly so much fun."

-- John Volker, *Lawyer, author and fly fisherman.*

Analyzing fishing spots. "Fish seem to be in places where it is easy to survive, be undisturbed, and can access get food. Fish moving water if you can. Moving water brings little mouthfuls of food for fish waiting for them.

"If you are near rocks or a drop-off where the water is rippling over them, you will be better off letting your fly drift with the current. Why? The water will be deeper on the downstream side of the rocks due to the turbulence caused by them and the water accelerating to get over them. And the water will be calmer there, less current, etc. The predators will sit there and wait for the current to bring them dinner. It makes for an easy dinner with less energy expended not fighting the current. In the summer deeper water is cooler water, and look for any trees shading the pool behind the rocks, etc."

-- Anon.

Nature of time. "Time is but the stream I go a-fishing in. Its thin current slides away, but eternity remains."

> -- Henry David Thoreau

Essentials. "Time flies so fast after youth is past that we cannot accomplish one half the many things we have in mind or indeed one half our duties.

"The only safe and sensible plan is to make other things give way to the essentials, and the first of these is fly fishing."

> -- Theodore Gordon

A few reasons for fly-fishing.

- Fresh fish on the dinner table. You are eating fish you caught that day, not fish that have been caught or raised on a farm and shipped halfway around the world. The flavor of truly fresh fish is something that only anglers and their friends and family members usually get to experience.

- The simple act of being outdoors and enjoying the sun and the trees and the wind and the waves and the rain and whatever else mother nature provides.

- The hunt. First, you need to find the fish, then you need to determine what they are eating. This takes an intimate knowledge of the habits of the species you are hunting and of the various differences between the environments they are in.

- The anticipation. Often 90 and sometimes 100 percent of your casts come up empty. You can cast all day and not catch a thing. On a good day, perhaps 10–15 percent of your casts will result in a hookup. You never know which cast and you will never know how big or small the fish is until you get it to your side.

- The challenge. Some fish are particularly hard to catch (wild trout for instance) and the right fly, properly presented can increase your chances of catching one of those more difficult to fool fish.

- The skills. Fly fishing requires skills and learning about insects (entomology) will help you. Learn their life cycles. It is important to understand their various cycles will speed up your overall comprehension along with catching more fish. Fly anglers are half-scientists and half-fishermen.

- Hunting. Understand that learning about fly fishing is to hunt fish and increase your chance of catching them which usually increases over a lifetime.

Unrewarded? "Unless one can enjoy himself fishing with the fly, even when his efforts are unrewarded, he loses much real pleasure. More than half the intense enjoyment of fly-fishing is derived from the beautiful surroundings, the satisfaction felt from being in the open air, the new lease of life secured thereby, and the many, many pleasant recollections of all one has seen, heard and done."

> -- Charles F. Orvis, 1886

Old saying. "Give a man a fish, and he'll eat for a day.

Give a fish a man, and he'll eat for weeks!"

> -- Toshihiro Kawabata

Farthest cast into a fishbowl. Maria Dolores Montesinos Fernández (Spain) holds the world record when she cast a weighted fly into a fishbowl with a neck diameter of 17.5 cm (6.8 in) without touching the sides from 7 m (22.96 ft) at the studios of El Show de los Récords, Madrid, Spain on 11 December 2001. [11]

A few fish puns.

Q. Why did the trout leave the cult?

A. They were too sacrifishal

Q. Something tastes funny!

A. That must be the clownfish.

Q. Aren't you going to eat your sushi?

A. Sorry, but it looks fishy.

Q. How do fish keep up with things?

A. They listen to current news.

Q. Why did the teenage fish get told off in school?

A. Because he was talking on his shell phone.

Q. What happens when you mix a fish and a banker?

A. A loan shark.

Q. Why do fish swim in schools?

A. Because they can't walk.

Q. What fish travels 100 mph?

A. A motor pike.

Q. Why couldn't the fisherman learn to read?

A. He was lost at C.

(I can't think of any more fish puns. I just flounder... well, then again, I'll mullet over.)

World Record for the largest Brook Trout. This is the second-oldest world record in the IGFA books, and a Dr. Cook set this record over 100 years ago. It is also several pounds heavier than the next heaviest brook trout that IGFA has ever documented. It was caught by Dr. J. W. Cook in 1915 and weighed 14 pounds 8 ounces.

Honesty. "Fly fishermen are born honest, but they get over it."

   -- Ed Zern

Looking over your shoulder. "Somebody just back of you while you are fishing is as bad as someone looking over your shoulder while you write a letter to your girl."

   -- Ernest Hemingway

World records for the largest bass. The small mouth bass world record is 11 pounds 15 ounces caught by David Hayes in Dale Hallow Lake, Tennessee. The next closest fish to his record is a 10-pound 14-ounce fish caught from the same lake in 1969.

The World Record Largemouth Bass is 22 Pounds 4 Ounces, and 22 Pounds 5 Ounces (a tie since IGFA requires at least a 2 oz difference to break a world record for fish weighing less than 25 pounds). George W. Perry caught his 22-pound, 4-ounce largemouth in 1932. This record stood for over 70 years. In 2009, Manabu Kurita caught a bass that weighed 22 pounds 5 ounces in Japan's Lake Biwa.

Many loves. "I have many loves and fly fishing is one of them. It brings peace and harmony to my being, which I can then pass on to others."

-- Sue Kreutzer

Fishing for compliments. I'm not good at fishing for compliments. All I get is trout.

Some of the largest fish caught on flyrods. The
IGFA maintains the World Records for species of game fish. [12]
You can search all IGFA World Records for freshwater and
saltwater fish species in All-Tackle Line Class, All-Tackle
Length for male, female and junior anglers. You can also
download the application to submit a potential record, learn
about scale certification, pretest your fishing line, and more.

Ever wonder about the largest fish ever caught on a fly rod?
These are just some of the details of fish caught that would be
amazing catches on any kind of tackle, but these catches are
even more remarkable since they were caught on a fly rod. Here
are just some of them in alphabetical order. [13]

Albacore Tuna. 47 POUNDS by Robert Lubarsky of Effort,
Pennsylvania caught in Hudson Canyon, off New Jersey in
September 1992 using a fly. It took him 20 minutes to land the
tuna.

Great Barracuda 60 pounds by Jodie L. Johnson of
Peterborough, New Hampshire at the Cosmoledo Atoll,
Seychelles in December 2005 and the fight time was 8 minutes.

Striped Bass. 64 pounds, 8 Ounces by Beryl Bliss of Fallon,
Nevada in the Smith River, Oregon in July 1973.

Cobia 83 Pounds, 4 Ounces by Jim Anson of Miami, Florida
off Key West, Florida in January 1986. Fight time 2 hours.

Dolphin fish (Mahi Mahi) 32 Pounds, 8 Ounces by Jodie L. Johnson of Peterborough, New Hampshire in the Bahamas in April 2006 and fight time was only 1 minute.

Red Drum 41 Pounds by Jim Seegraves of Tampa, Florida in Houma, Louisiana in April 2003 and fight time was 1 hour and 55 minutes. to land it.

Pacific Halibut 138 Pounds by Jim Seegraves of Tampa, Florida in Icy Bay, Alaska in July 2008, and fight time was 1 hour 15 minutes.

Horse-eye Jack 25 Pounds by Hermann Fehringer of Lenggries, Germany off of Ascension Island in April 2002 and the fight time was 23 minutes.

King Mackerel 51 Pounds, 4 Ounces by Rick Gunion of Palmetto Bay, Florida off of Key West, Florida in February 1987. The fight time was 31 minutes.

Blue Marlin 288 Pounds by Thomas M. Evans, Jr. of Wilson, Wyoming in Port Stephens, Australia in March 2002, and the fight time was 1 hour.

Striped Marlin 97 Pounds by Tony Hedley off Cabo San Lucas, Mexico in December 2000. Fight time 1 hour 15 minutes.

Permit 41 Pounds by Del Brown of Watsonville, California off Key West, Florida in March 1986. Fight time 1 hour 3 minutes.

Pollock (Coalfish) 28 Pounds 14 Ounces by Kritian Keskitalo in Norway in August 2021. Fight time 20 minutes.

Talang Queenfish 35 Pounds, 4 Ounces.

Roosterfish 60 Pounds caught by Margaret Shaughnessy of Medford, Oregon in Punta Las Arenas, Mexico, June 2013 using a Raton fly and a long fight time of 3 hours, 40 minutes.

Rainbow Runner 18 Pounds, 3 Ounces by Frank C. Carter off Challenger Bank, Bermuda, June 2006.

Pacific Sailfish 136 Pounds by Stu Apte off Piñas Bay, Panama. June 1965

Tiger Shark 490 Pounds by Rick Gunion off Matanilla Shoal, The Bahamas with a fight time of 40 minutes, March 2008.

Red Snapper 26 Pounds, 9 Ounces by Doug Borries in the Gulf of Mexico off Mississippi, October 2013 with a fight time of 15 minutes.

Swordfish 89 Pounds, 15 Ounces by Fouad Sahioui off Casablanca, Morocco with a fight time of 25 minutes.

Tarpon 202 Pounds, 8 Ounces by James Holland in Chassahowitzka, Florida, May 2001 with a fight time of 1 hour 50 minutes.

Dogtooth Tuna 147 Pounds, 14 Ounces by H. T. Chittum III at the Great Barrier Reef, Australia in October 2005. Fight time 35 minutes.

Yellowfin Tuna 107 Pounds, 2 Ounces by Trevor M. Hansen off Cape Town, South Africa in February 2006 on a sardine fly with a long fight time of 4 hours, 45 minutes.

Wahoo 77 Pounds, 2 Ounces by David Long at Banks Island, Vanuatu in February 2006 with a fight time of 3 hours, 10 minutes on a red wahoo fly.

That one that got away. "In every species of fish I've angled for, it is the ones that have got away that thrill me the most, the ones that keep fresh in my memory.

"So, I say it is good to lose fish...

"If we didn't, much of the thrill of angling would be gone."

-- Ray Bergman

Smoked trout flavored ice cream? A January 1994 Reuters News Service story on Manuel Oliveira's ice cream shop in Merida, Venezuela, reported on his 567 flavors, including onion, chili, beer, eggplant, **smoked trout**, spaghetti parmesan, chicken with rice, and spinach. Manuel said some flavors fail and he once abandoned avocado ice cream, and tossed out 99 pounds of it, because it wasn't smooth enough.

Can't hide. "Creeps and idiots cannot conceal themselves for long on a fishing trip."

-- John Gierach

Three blondes and the Game Warden. Three blondes are sitting by the side of a river holding fishing poles with the lines in the water.

A Game Warden comes up behind them, taps them on the shoulder and says, "Excuse me, ladies, I'd like to see your fishing licenses."

"We don't have any," replied the first blonde.

"Well, if you're going to fish, you need fishing licenses," said the Game Warden.

"But officer," replied the second blonde, "we aren't fishing. We all have magnets at the end of our lines and we're collecting debris off the bottom of the river."

The Game Warden lifted all the lines and, sure enough, there were horseshoe magnets tied on the end of each line. "Well, I know of no law against it," said the Game Warden. "Take all the debris you want." And with that, he left.

As soon as the Game Warden was out of sight, the three blondes started laughing hysterically. "What a dumb Fish Cop," the second blonde said to the other two. "Doesn't he know that there are steelhead trout in this river?"

Fish sounds. Fish produce different types of low-pitched sounds to communicate with each other. But fish don't have vocal cords but use different body parts are used to create noises, like pulsating their muscles against their swim bladder.

A few trout fly fishing facts. [14]

- The first ever recorded instance of fly-fishing was in early Rome when Roman writer Claudius Aelianus described the fishers on the river using flies to catch their prey in 200 A.D.

- Trout can live in a water temperature range between 32 and about 70 degrees, but they're most at home in waters that are around 55 to 60 degrees.

- A few larger New Zealand trout have even been known to nab the occasional mouse.

- Salmon and trout are in the same family. In recent years, naturalists have noticed that farm-bred salmon who escaped and certain types of trout are breeding with one another.

- Pregnant trout can lay as many as 900 eggs per pound of body weight every time they spawn. Around the age of three or four, they'll start their own spawning.

- Trout can live up to 20 years.

- Trout have excellent vision. They can focus their vision on two different targets simultaneously, and their eyes' range of motion essentially allows them 360-degree vision.

- For about the first month of their life, baby trout have no scales.

- Bottom or surface feeders? Both. But most trout are surface feeders, which means most skim the surface for insects.

The American Museum of Fly Tying is a museum in Manchester, Vermont, United States, which preserves and exhibits artifacts related to American angling. [15] The Museum serves as conservator of the world's largest collection of angling and angling-related items, numbering in the thousands.

The collections and exhibits document the evolution of fly fishing as a sport, art form, craft, and industry in the United States and abroad, dating as far back as the sixteenth century. Rods, reels, flies, tackle, art, photographs, manuscripts, and books form the Museum's permanent collection, including the oldest documented flies in the world. [16]

It is located at 4104 Main Street, Manchester, Vermont 05254 and was established in the 1960s.

Te awa o te Atua – The Creator's River. On New Zealand's North Island, there is a river called the Rangitikei River which is one of New Zealand's longest rivers being 157 miles long. [17]

Its headwaters are to the southeast of Lake Taupō in the Kaimanawa Ranges. It flows from the Central Plateau south past Taihape, Mangaweka, Hunterville, Marton, and Bulls, to the South Taranaki Bight at Tangimoana, 25 miles southeast of Whanganui. The river gives its name to the surrounding Rangitikei District. [18]

Our Māori guide who led us told us this river has been known as "The Creator's River" since it was believed that it was created by God to use anytime He wanted to fly fish."

When we arrived at the first spot, we could see how the river got its name as the natural beauty certainly gave us the impression this was a holy place with crystal blue-green waters where rainbows could be seen clearly through four feet of the pure crystal clear waters.

The fish ranged from 6 to 11 pounds due to huge hatches of aquatic insects. The trout grow large from them as well as a variety of caddis, mayflies, ants, and beetles.

People such as Presidents Bush & Clinton and many celebrities come from all over the world to fly fish and experience this unspoiled land and hopefully, it will remain that way in future years. There are many pristine and natural rivers to explore in this magical land.

Fish can drown. Fish require oxygen just like we do and may suffocate if there is not enough amount of oxygen in the water that they live in. [19]

Seventeen reasons why fishing is better than sex...

1. You don't have to hide your Fishing magazines.

2. It is perfectly acceptable to pay a professional to fish with you occasionally.

3. The Ten Commandments don't say anything about fishing.

4. If your partner takes pictures or videotapes of you fishing, you don't have to worry about them showing up on the internet if you become famous.

5. Your fishing partner doesn't get upset about people you fished with long ago.

6. It's perfectly respectable to fish with a total stranger.

7. When you see a good fisherperson, you don't have to feel guilty about imagining the two of you fishing together.

8. If your regular fishing partner isn't available, he/she won't object if you fish with someone else.

9. Nobody will ever tell you that you will go blind if you fish by yourself.

10. You can have a fishing calendar on your wall at the office, tell fishing jokes, and invite coworkers to fish with you without getting sued for harassment.

11. Your fishing partner will never say, "Not again? We just fished last week! Is fishing all you ever think about?"

12. When you go fishing and you catch something, that's good. If you're making love and you catch something, that's bad.

13. Fish don't compare you to other fishermen and fish don't want to know how many other fish you caught.

14. In fishing, you lie about the one that got away. In love, you lie to still be friends after you let it go.

15. You don't have to necessarily change your line to keep catching fish.

16. You can catch a fish on a 20-cent nightcrawler. If you want to catch a woman you're talking dinner and a movie minimum.

17. Fish don't mind if you fall asleep in the middle of fishing.

An old one - The Fishing Trip. On Friday afternoon, a man calls home to his wife and says, "Honey I have been asked to go on a fishing trip with my boss. We'll be gone a week. This is a great chance for me to work on that promotion! Would you please pack some clothes for me and set out my rod and tackle box? I'll swing by the house to pick them up in an hour. Oh! And please pack my new blue pajamas."

The wife thinks this sounds a little fishy but does exactly what her husband asked.

The following weekend the husband comes home very tired, tan and happy. The wife welcomes him home and asks if he has had a good time.

"I did!" he says as he carries his things into the bedroom. "You wouldn't believe all the fish we caught! Some bass, some catfish, and a few trout."

As he tosses his suitcase onto the bed, his wife leans against the doorjamb.

"Really?" She asks.

"Yup," he says. Then he glances up at her, "By the way, why didn't you pack my new blue pajamas like I asked?"

The wife crosses her arms and replies, "I did. They're in your tackle box."

Peace. "There is certainly something in angling that tends to produce a serenity of mind."

-- Washington Irving

Did you evolve into becoming a fly fisherman?
If so, can you relate to this story?

"I started fly fishing after small water bass fishing from my canoe got boring—I realized I was only having fun doing it throwing frogs on lily pads or over slop, and then with the gear required to do that, there's no real fight. Plus, I wanted something I could do for a bit when I had my car (but not the canoe) at college. I started with dry flies and buggers; I like tradition and I also like catching fish.

"I met a guy on a tiny little central MA stream, fishing a bamboo rod he built, and he got a 14" brown I'd been going for over an hour on his first cast. I realized how much I didn't know and had a chance to witness some exquisite matching of gear to the environment—I didn't ask for the specs, but that rod couldn't have been over 6'6", and at that time the shortest rod I had was 8'6".

"I remember the first trout I ever got to eat a #30 fly, and all the #28s he passed up before that. I remember making a streamside mono rig before I knew what it was to try and get a streamer down fast in fast water, and the total surprise of picking up my first walleye on the fly when it worked.

"Over the years—I've only been at this a bit over a decade— I've found myself occupying a sort of post-Halford Ian position in the philosophy of my fishing. I adore dry fly fishing, but I find myself equally satisfied by presenting a fly that suits the environment. Tiny midges on tailwaters make sense. A tiny black wet fly when swarms of tiny black caddies are in the air (and the fish won't touch the dries) makes sense.

"I also use spey-style crayfish patterns for smallmouth in rivers make sense. I'm becoming more of a generalist, but also finding myself caring more about how I catch the fish. I've found that I love pursuing big sunfish and bluegill, but I'm only going after them in rivers, even though I know lakes where they get bigger. I care about catching the fish in the places and the ways that I love.

"I also appreciate some opportunities the sport has for weirdness and targeting non-traditional species. I'm looking forward to the spring and a chance at targeting carp in the shallows of a nearby lake. There's a river with a big run of impressively sized suckers in some deep and fast water—I'm hoping to take shots at euro nymphing for them. Similarly, I've been wondering about using euro nymphing strategies for some fast runs and pockets in river sections with big fallfish and smallmouth.

"Lastly, I can't shake the environmentalist view of it all. Sometimes I think maybe I stray away from trout out of a blend of guilt, fear, and hopefulness. Here in Mass, we stock so many unsustainable trout populations, fail to manage waters that support stream-born populations, and generally do a poor job of supporting the natural resources in a way that prioritizes their permanence and self-sufficiency over our short-term enjoyment.

"I don't watch to catch a stocker rainbow to forget that we're burning down the planet—I'd rather enjoy catching a smallmouth just downstream of a power plant and grapple with the reality that this is the world we built for ourselves."

– Anon.

A toast after fishing.

Here's to our fisherman bold,

Here's to the fish he CAUGHT,

Here's to the one that got away,

And here's to the one he BOUGHT.

The Essentials of a Good Fly-Hook: "The temper of an angel and penetration of a prophet; fine enough to be invisible and strong enough to kill a bull in a ten-acre field."

> -- G.S. Marryat, *1840- 1896 "Prince of Fly Fishers"* *Influential in developing dry-fly fishing on the chalk streams of southern England with F. M. Halford.*

Unlucky? No way! "I've gone fishing thousands of times in my life, and I have never once felt unlucky or poorly paid for those hours on the water."

> -- William G. Tapply

Fishing with the wife. Alan takes his wife fishing and on a usual trip, he catches 10-15 fish. He's amazed when the pair of them manage a haul of over 100!

So, he decided to enter them both into the local fishing competition.

The day of the competition rolls around. The first man is a big beefy lad, and he catches 5 fish.

The second is a woman in her 30s, typical American heroine-plaid jacket, and platinum blonde hair. She manages to catch 17 fish, and it looks like the competition is already over.

Finally, Alan is up. As usual, he only catches 15 fish, which is still good for him. He walks past his competitors, beaming.

"Why are you so happy?" They ask him.

"My wife is up next, and she's sure to win!"

The other competitors laugh, they've seen his wife. She's in her 50s, tight permed hair and with a little apron, the pinnacle of domesticity, looking like she's never fished in her life.

To their surprise, she catches 250 fish! The competition is called off due to concerns for local wildlife, and everyone is surrounding Alan and his wife wanting to know how she did it. Also, there's a reporter from the local paper there who wants to do a story on the amazing event and says, "Who are you amazing Anglers?"

"I'm Alan, and this is my Wife."

"And what's her name?"

"Annette."

God created Canada. On the 6th day, God turned to Archangel Gabriel and said: "Today I am going to create a land called Canada, and it will be a land of outstanding natural beauty. It shall have tall, majestic mountains, beautiful sparkling lakes bountiful with bass and trout, forests full of elk and moose, high cliffs over-looking sandy beaches with an abundance of sea life, and rivers stocked with salmon."

God continued, "I shall make the land rich in oil so as to make the inhabitants prosper, I shall call these inhabitants Canadians, and they shall be known as the most friendly and kindest people on the earth."

"But Lord," asked Gabriel, "Don't you think you are being too generous to these Canadians?"

"Not really," replied God, "Just wait until I make their neighbors."

Best time to fish. "The two best times to fish is when it's rainin' and when it ain't."

-- Patrick F. McManus, *Humorist*

Equality. "To go fishing is the chance to wash one's soul with pure air, with the rush of the brook, or with the shimmer of sun on blue water.

"It brings meekness and inspiration from the decency of nature, charity toward tackle-makers, patience toward fish, a mockery of profits and egos, a quieting of hate, a rejoicing that you do not have to decide a darned thing until next week.

"And it is discipline in the equality of men - for all men are equal before fish."

-- Herbert Hoover

Worms. "There is no greater fan of fly-fishing than the worm."

-- Patrick F. McManus, *"Never Sniff a Gift Fish,"* 1979

More fish puns.

Q. Why will fish never take responsibility?

A. Because it's always salmon else's fault.

Q. Why did the shopkeeper throw the clams out?

A. They were past their shell-by-date.

Q. What type of instrument do fish love to play?

A. A bass drum.

Q. Why did the fish start a charity?

A. He was reely good at finraising.

Q. Why don't fish go into business together?

A. They are always sole traders.

Q. Why do fish not go to war?

A. Because they are paci-fish-ts.

Moment of beauty. "A trout is a moment of beauty known only to those who seek it."

-- Arnold Gingrich, *Co-founder of Esquire Magazine and accomplished fly fisherman.*

Philosophers. "Scholars have long known that fishing eventually turns men into philosophers. Unfortunately, it is almost impossible to buy decent tackle on a philosopher's salary."

-- Patrick F. McManus

Overly hungry. "Hmm," I said to the fishmonger, examining the selection. "I've got the munchies. I will eat any of these."

"Smoked trout?" he asked.

"No," I replied. "Just a little bit of weed."

Brain workers. "Fly-fishers are usually brain workers in society. Along the banks of purling streams, beneath the shadows of umbrageous trees, or in the secluded nooks of charming lakes, they have ever been found, drinking deep of the invigorating forces of nature - giving rest and tone to over-taxed brains and wearied nerves - while gracefully wielding the supple rod, the invisible leader, and the fairy-like fly."

-- James A. Hensall, MD, 1855

Trout farms. "Stocked trout are as wild as a Chihuahua sitting in a pink velvet handbag."

— Fennel Hudson

Charmed. "The charm of fishing is that it is the pursuit of what is elusive but attainable, a perpetual series of occasions for hope."

-- John Buchan

Add bacon. "Trout plus bacon is one of civilization's greatest formulas; it always equals pleasure."

-- Jonathan Miles

Scotland. "If you're trout fishing in the lochs of Scotland, your catch may end up like this: batter-crusted with that ubiquitous Scottish staple, oats; and served beside a generous mound of stovies, Scottish slang for stove-roasted potatoes."

-- Jonathan Miles

Rising to the sky. "When a trout rises to a fly, it does not swim as much as tilt its fins and jet skyward."

-- Joseph Monninger, *Writer and Professor of English at Plymouth State University*

Still with me. "The trout is still with me, as are my memories. The future is somewhere between these two forces, but it lives in mystery. The river records to trail behind or before me and covers everything as it flows. This mountain and this river are old, yet as I wade alone, they both appear young and new to me."

— Daniel J. Rice, *The Unpeopled Season: Journal from a North Country Wilderness*

Mystery. "Once there were brook trout in the streams in the mountains. You could see them standing in the amber current where the white edges of their fins wimpled softly in the flow. They smelled of moss in your hand. Polished and muscular and torsional. On their backs were vermiculate patterns that were maps of the world in its becoming. Maps and mazes. Of a thing which could not be put back. Not be made right again. In the deep glens where they lived all things were older than man and they hummed of mystery."

— Cormac McCarthy, *The Road*

Grand scheme. "...they say you forget your troubles on a trout stream, but that's not quite it. What happens is that you begin to see where your troubles fit into the grand scheme of things, and suddenly they're just not such a big deal anymore."

-- John Gierach, *Author*

Final thoughts. "So, get out there and hunt and fish and mess around with your friends, ramble out yonder and explore the forests, climb the mountains, bag the peaks, run the rivers, breathe deep of that yet sweet and lucid air, sit quietly for a while and contemplate the precious stillness, the lovely, mysterious, and awesome space."

— Derek Grzelewski, *Writer*

We hope you enjoyed our book!

If you liked our book, we would sincerely appreciate your taking a few moments to leave a brief review.

Thank you again very much!

TeamGolfwell and Bruce Miller

Bruce@TeamGolfwell.com

About the authors

Bruce Miller. Lawyer, businessman, world traveler, golf enthusiast, Golf Rules Official, actor, whiskey connoisseur, and author of over 40 books, a few being Amazon bestsellers, spends his days writing, studying, and constantly learning of the astounding, unexpected, and amazing events happening in the world today while exploring the brighter side of life. He is a member of Team Golfwell, Authors, and Publishers.

TeamGolfwell are bestselling authors and founders of the very popular 230,000+ member Facebook Group "Golf Jokes and Stories." Their books have sold thousands of copies including several #1 bestsellers in Golf Coaching, Sports humor, and other categories.

We Want to Hear from You!

"There usually is a way to do things better and there is opportunity when you find it." - Thomas Edison

We love to hear your thoughts and suggestions on anything and please feel free to contact us at
Bruce@TeamGolfwell.com

Other Books by Bruce Miller [20] and Team Golfwell [21]

Brilliant Screen-Free Stuff to Do with Kids: A Handy Reference for Parents & Grandparents!

For the Golfer Who Has Everything: A Funny Golf Book

For the Mother Who Has Everything: A Funny Book for Mother

For the Father Who Has Everything: A Funny Book for Father

For the Grandmother Who Has Everything: A Funny Book for Grandmothers

For the Grandfather Who Has Everything: A Funny Book for Grandfathers

The Funniest Quotations to Brighten Every Day: Brilliant, Inspiring, and Hilarious Thoughts from Great Minds

Jokes for Very Funny Kids (Ages 3 to 7): Funny Jokes, Riddles and More

Jokes for Very Funny Kids (Big & Little): Funny Jokes and Riddles Ages 9 - 12 and up and many more. [22]

And many more…

Index

References

[1] Flydreamers, https://www.flydreamers.com/en/history-of-fly-fishing

[2] Wikipedia, https://en.wikipedia.org/wiki/Fly_fishing#:~:text=In%20the%20late%2019th%20century,the%20Beaverkill%20and%20Willowemoc%20Creek.

[3] Ibid.

[4] Wikipedia, https://en.wikipedia.org/wiki/Fly_line

[5] Wikipedia, https://en.wikipedia.org/wiki/Fly_fishing

[6] Wikipedia, https://en.wikipedia.org/wiki/Orvis

[7] Wikipedia, https://en.wikipedia.org/wiki/Favorite_Flies_and_Their_Histories

[8] Wikipedia, World Fly Fishing Championship, https://en.wikipedia.org/wiki/World_Fly_Fishing_Championships

[9] Ibid.

[10] Guinness World Records, https://www.guinnessworldrecords.com/world-records/64839-fly-fishing-world-champs-team

[11] Guinness World Records, https://www.guinnessworldrecords.com/world-records/fly-fishing-farthest-cast-into-a-fish-bowl

[12] IGFA World Records, https://igfa.org/world-records/

[13] Ibid.

[14] Wikipedia, https://en.wikipedia.org/wiki/Trout

[15] Wikipedia, https://en.wikipedia.org/wiki/American_Museum_of_Fly_Fishing

[16] Ibid.
[17] Wikipedia, Rangitikei River,
https://en.wikipedia.org/wiki/Rangit%C4%ABkei_River
[18] Ibid.
[19] Socratic.org, https://socratic.org/questions/what-happens-if-fish-do-not-have-enough-dissolved-oxygen
[20] https://www.amazon.com/Bruce-Miller/e/B096C9SN2R?
[21] https://www.amazon.com/Team-Golfwell/e/B01CFW4EQG?
[22] Ibid.

Printed in Great Britain
by Amazon

27226792R00057